Under The Influence

by

Louise G Cole

First published 2022 by The Hedgehog Poetry Press

Published in the UK by
The Hedgehog Poetry Press
5, Coppack House
Churchill Avenue
Clevedon
BS21 6QW

www.hedgehogpress.co.uk

ISBN: 978-1-913499-50-1

Copyright © Louise G Cole 2022

The right of Louise G Cole to be identified as the author of this work has been asserted in accordance with the Copyright, Designs and Patents Act 1988.

All rights reserved. No part of this publication may be reproduced, stored in or introduced into a retrieval system, or transmitted in any form, or by any means (electronic, mechanical, photocopying, recording or otherwise) without prior written permissions of the publisher. Any person who does any unauthorised act in relation to this publication may be liable for criminal prosecution and civil claims for damages.

9 8 7 6 5 4 3 2 1

A CIP Catalogue record for this book is available from the British Library.

Cover Image based upon a painting © Sinéad Foley Coleman

Contents

Learning to Sew 5
PC in the Sixties 6
Reality Check 7
Recalling Wash Day Dinners 8
Kelvin Road, Still Flying Solo 9
Fur Coat and No Knickers 10
Breaking, Sad 11
Twinkle Toes 12
Universal Truth 13
Gift 14
After the Care Home Displays Contempt for Knick-Knacks 15
May Time 16
Labelling my Mother 17
To the Drinker of Cabbage Water: 18
One November Night, My Mother Dies 19
Origami Instructions for the Recently Bereaved 20
Piccalilli Stains Yellow 22
Still More Onions to Chop 23
That. Wooden. Spoon. 24
Under the Influence 25
Walking the Back Road, After 26

Learning to Sew

She stitched me right into childhood,
paper pattern pieces of maternal advice
from *The People's Friend, My Weekly,
Woman and Home*, invisible threads
- no-one should see crooked seams -
embroidered elaborate falsehoods,
basted ill-fitting words for my supper,
appliquéd subliminal messages, said
out loud I had a face only a mother
could love.

Believing, I took youth's sharp scissors,
hacked at gauche, awkward tacking,
unpicked mother and daughter outfits,
discovered I could sew my own dresses,
girl into woman shouting down rough
fabric, frayed raw edges, sagging hems,
I tailored new garments, gathered then
how to needle, needle, pinned all hope
on a tapestry of need she didn't expect
me to get.

PC in the Sixties

My mother stuck straw
in her hair held in place
with lacquer, smeared
pale cheeks with mascara
(the kind you spat on),
tied my dad's de-mob coat
with string wound twice,
to go to a tramp's supper,
raucous, wild, giggling
with her good friend Iris
from down the road.

Fancy dress fundraising
for respectable good causes,
she won first prize, came
home proud with a warm
bottle of white Blue Nun
and a pretty china tea set.

Now, I have one of the little
brown and orange side plates,
sitting in quiet apology
on my 21st century shelf,
a reminder of times when
next door's cat, black but
not sooty, was named Nigger,
when the homeless
were called tramps
and could be parodied
by jolly, middle-class ladies
from the WI.

Reality Check

Don't look said my mother
as the other kids gawped at
the dead dog in the gutter
See the rainbows, she whispered
pointing to oil-slicked puddles.
She talked fables and fairies and fluff
standing between me and reality,
hadn't heard Hemingway
describe an unhappy childhood
as the best early training for a writer.

Recalling Wash Day Dinners

Mondays always smelt wet, of hard-boiled whites
and gravy, cold kitchen windows blurred blind
by steam, my handle-turning mother grinding

yesterday's roast to mince, Shepherd's Pie made
savoury with crumbled Oxo cubes, her restless
fingers worn raw from caustic soda, borax, graft,

while we played outside, stayed scarce 'til tea-time,
listening for her shout, calling us back home to
long-boiled cabbage, carrot coins and tinned peas.

These days, my week starts with button-pressing
as I adjust the central heating, unload tumble-dried
rose-and-lavender laundry, scan freezer shelves

for ready meals, something eco-friendly from M & S
with nutritious aubergines, organic pomegranates,
quinoa, spiced and fragrant. I'll send a casual group

text *'Dinner's ready in five',* watch the microwave
turntable spin, might sniff the air and wonder, did
my mother ever notice this day had a certain smell?

Kelvin Road, Still Flying Solo

The heavy wrought-iron gate from 39a
to 40b swings six-year-old pre-sister me,
languid, loose-ended after Sunday Mass,
clean cotton-frocked, on promise of death
if any grime crimes emerge before lunch.

Kelvin Road's red bricks invite rhythm:

clang, bang, clang, humming in A Minor,
Janet Reesby, open-windowed upstairs
trying to perfect Für Elise, her mother
keeping time, chop, chop, chopping mint
for their roasted lamb dinner for two.

Downstairs, my mum is loudly, roundly

pounding pastry for pies, wondering
how much longer? as my father sharpens
knives, imagining a fine son, unprepared
for the disappointment heralded overhead
by a herringbone sky, as one mid-March day

everything, everything, everything changes.

Fur Coat and No Knickers

Drawing breath between tales of dead
        little brothers and elderly neighbours
moved away, my mother looks inside
        a lifetime that's 92 and counting,
claims no-one's visited for months,
        thinks I'm her cousin Betty
with designs on her fur coat and hopes
        of borrowing a fiver.
I try not to mind the Care Home smell
        and wonder what else to talk about when
the devil himself taps my shoulder
        suggests I unburden, reveal secrets
never before shared, so I offer a revelation:
        I lost my virginity four times
before I was married. She's never yet listened to me
        so it's no surprise she doesn't hear,
continues with a rattle about imagined walks
        in the park yesterday, shopping
trips she'll make next week.
        A carer comes to tuck her in,
brings weak tea and egg sandwiches,
        asks if I'd like some,
is relieved when I decline.
        I get up to leave and the frail old cripple
who used to be my mother
        spills her tea and demands
to know when cousin Betty intends returning
        the fur coat, says quietly: "I always knew
what a little whore you were".

Breaking, Sad

The 93-year-old cripple who used to be my mother
slips deeper into the oblivion of a Care Home chair
further from my reach than ever before,
the distance measured not only in miles.

When there's no news, I imagine some: miracle
cures and time-slips, back to hearty good health,
days when she jumped up to touch elderly toes
to impress strangers, look at me, look at me.

How long now since she enquired after my life,
in another country, her grandchildren respecting
state visits, good table manners, set bedtimes,
Nana soup, green, nutritious, compulsory?

It's hard to believe she told little me, all freckles
and wild ginger curls, mine was a face only
a mother could love. I have to think she did
 - would now if she could remember how -
because I kept all her letters, each one signed

with all my love
with all my love
with all my love.

Twinkle Toes

She'd like to dance
hears Benny Goodman braiding
time's open-ended funnel into a cocked ear,
wireless airwaves in a cat's cradle memory,
94 and counting.

She'd like to dance
the music overriding
Care Home slumps and groans,
forced cheeriness from carers,
yesterday's greens still simmering in the hall,
posters boasting home comforts.

She'd like to dance
with legs no longer working, still,
feet can twitch and toes, she smiles
for handsome wartime pilots,
garrulous, persuasive,
neat and uniformed.

She'd like to dance
the glamour days,
in kitten heels, parachute silk
and blood red lipstick,
rationing, hardships, lost
friends left unremarked.

She'd like to dance
beyond a lifetime shoe-horned into
an antiseptic box, top floor, first left,
and when Glen Miller's In The Mood
she breathes softly, keeping time,
keeping going.
She liked to dance.

Universal Truth

I didn't know I was the whole world,
the sun, the moon and the stars,
to my father until he was gone.

My mother mentioned it once
draping the news around her neck
as if it was a shawl to keep out draughts
shaking her head, aghast at his duplicity.

Gift

I bought delicate ladies' handkerchiefs
pretty pastel shades in fine cotton lawn
embroidered with tiny blue forget-me-nots
soft spun squares of nostalgia presented
in a beribboned box and it wasn't even
Mothering Sunday or her birthday, or mine –
then I remembered.

I couldn't give them to her, or mention them,
fearing the glaucous veil of Care Home sedation
might slip from her grasp and she might, if only
in one sad moment, realise what she's missing,
understand that every item in her closet
must be approved for the communal laundry,
marked in indelible ink with her name,
knowing only paper tissues are allowed there
to mop the tears.

After the Care Home Displays Contempt for Knick-Knacks

My mother's collected clutter plays Big Band tunes
on my maudlin streak, Glen Millers me into the mood
for hoarding, keeper of chipped Wedgwood, guardian
of gaudy, bent brass brooches, tatty tin trinkets.

Already, I'm sentimental sentry to saggy, baggy sweaters,
hand-knitted, never fashionable, ever unworn, forlorn,
stored not in apologetic heaps for the charity bin
but bin-bagged in the attic, under eaves where space

struggles to catch its breath, invites in mice to party,
rats, bats, woolly spiders as big as memories whisper
how this stuff isn't really junk, might one day prove
valuable, worth a bit, the leftovers of a long lifetime

not even mine,
and soon,
soon no longer hers either.

May Time

At May month start, we cast off April,
find bluebell woods in first blue bloom,

close on the crunch of last year's fallings
sunlight spangling the tops of our heads,

spring-thin branches only vaguely frilled
with promise of full-blown leaves above,

drifts of celandines, violets, wild orchids,
white sheets of musky wood anemones.

By May month end, air warms into June,
blossoms setting up autumn's fat fruit,

brick-thick leafed canopies above us,
bluebell carpets faded to grey green,

the lane's welcoming yellow corridor
of dandelions now turned to clocks,

reminding me, I'm too late to gather
armfuls of wild flowers for my mother.

Labelling my Mother

No more letters home can mark my fingers
with permanent ink, but still I streak black
a blank page, tracing long lines on paper
from my heart to her soul and back again.

I taste salt, know indelible ink will not wash
away with soap suds and water, only time
will fade marks in her clothes pen-labelled
with a name the sound of my initials: Elsie.

She never like the music of it, preferred
her teenage war-time badge referencing
flaming hair and matching temper: Ginger,
though my father called her his Duchess.

Some days she could out-bouquet the best
Hyacinth Bucket and woe betide the poor
tradesman or doctor's receptionist being
chummy and matey, first-name familiar.

So she was Mrs C, no-one's Darlin', or Else,
until such time my 94-year old care-homed
mother closed her eyes to visitors, stopped
reading letters, spoke only when she had to.

And when she thought no-one was watching,
she stared at the inky insignia attached to her
washable cardigan and flowery nightdress,
wondering aloud at all the wrong name labels.

To the Drinker of Cabbage Water:

I've changed my mind

Remembering dinner table battles-of-will over
meat and two veg, grey gravy congealing to fury,
you push, push, pushing little me, *eat the greens,*
claiming boiled cabbage good for me, enjoyable,
your pantomime of drinking - with relish - cold
salty cooking water, soft leafy shreds still afloat
as I gag, heave, bawl, forced to forfeit dessert,
maybe only once sent to bed early for defiance,
next day, last night's meal set out for breakfast,
stuff of family legend, recall skewed sideways
depending on who is telling the same old story.

Your surprise when later, we grew cabbages
football sized, cannonball heavy, as green as
you like, and now I do like, after all those years,
I realised cruciferous is delicious as well as good
for me, and I loved telling you I'm finally greened.

One November Night, My Mother Dies

A shape shifts in the doorway welcoming me home
Black Friday, darkest of days, the longest of nights.

I slam the car door, see a flinch as the sound echoes
across dust and dander dancing in the porchlight.

I suspect nothing more than concern for the lateness
of my arrival until he shares bad, sad news and then
and then
and then
all I can hear
all I can hear
is the soft wingbeat of winter moths, moths, moths,
trying to get to the light.

Origami Instructions for the Recently Bereaved

1. Fold your grief inwards from the corners to centre, into a shape not neat, precise or equally proportioned
2. Right side out, press along the creases with tenderness and care, tears (and tears) are inevitable in the early stages of this process but can be hidden with careful composure, stoicism, support, mindfulness, alcohol
3. Keeping raw patches of disbelief and despair well tucked in, carefully hold sides, press and pinch firmly to distribute the burden more evenly, remembering to keep breathing, keep breathing, keep breathing
4. If edges fray, express regret quietly and with decorum, turning deep sadness back to front when in public

5. In private, spread out the whole hurt, tracing along the edges of loneliness, anger, fear, permanent marks may fade eventually, but only with time. Time. Lots of time.
6. At this stage, your mandate for bitterness may require punching holes, unfurling crumpled parts, shredding, stamping, tearing strips, impromptu perforations
7. Understand nothing breaks like a heart, so it may be necessary to reassemble the pieces and start again, still remembering to breathe, to breathe, to breathe
8. Fold your grief inwards from the corners...

Piccalilli Stains Yellow

Each salt and malt vinegar September
we'd dust down the big Oxford Concise
to be sure, sure, sure she had the right
number of L, Cs and Is on lick-down
labels, glow-in-the-dark Kilners stacked,
deep-packed with cut-price cauliflower,
home-grown green beans, next door's
mis-shaped cucumbers, garden harvest
nasturtium seeds pushed home, fingers
tipped turmeric and mustard, pointing
to pantry top shelf, Christmas set-aside,
ahead of fifty years, when struck dumb
in the preserves and pickle aisle of Asda,
I come perilously close to *buying* Piccalilli.

Still More Onions to Chop

On the counter rests a battered book
opened at her long-kept favourites,
old pencilled recipes on pages I turn
for perfect pastry, French Onion Soup.

The vegetable rack sits close to hand
alongside the sharpest kitchen knives
colour-coordinated chopping boards,
strategically placed box of tissues.

When time doesn't heal but just passes,
I pick up an onion, begin the peeling
of papery layers, dry old skin giving
way to strong white flesh, unforgiving

unforgetting, I start to chop, then stop,
allow the sad scent to linger on fingers,
refuse the advice of well-wishers, plates
piled with platitudes, overdone clichés

crisp, ready-salted. I ignore suggestions
to burn candles, close eyes, hold breath,
work under water. They'll cluck, tut, look
forward to out of season onion marmalade,

relish, chutney, as I blame enzyme alliinase
lachrymatory-factor synthase, sulfenic acid
- more convincing than the truth, believable,
so long as I keep the onion net well-stocked.

That. Wooden. Spoon.

My mother, standing at the stove,
is eating porridge from the pan,
sprinkling it with salt as my father
gags his disapproval, his sweet tooth
demanding sugar, honey, syrup,
fresh first thing, hot, not cold and
eaten as left-overs at improper
times of the day or the night.

> *Waste not, want not,* she grins,
> her mouth gaping goo, waving,
> waving that old wooden spoon
> until Ciara from the Care Home
> comes to corral her back to bed.

When I challenge dream as memory
I fear the work of restless sleep
has managed to blend now with then,
the smacking lips slapping recall
into a bowl of grey gruel stirred angry
with that wooden, wooden spoon.

Under the Influence

Since you are no longer here to disapprove
I have taken to cursing aloud, in lewd, salty
language (I always knew the words, never
before felt the f-ing need to shout them).

While I'm at it, you should know I've stopped
going to Mass, hardly ever bother with side
plates and serviettes, now wear my hair long,
my skirts short, stay up long after midnight,

sleep in the next day, pass off shop-bought
pastry as my own, bin every sock with a hole,
have mislaid the button box, sometimes talk
with my mouth full, lean elbows on the table.

I don't keep in touch with the cousins, or your
last two sisters, sometimes waste my money
on take-outs, allow the dog to sit on the sofa,
talk loud enough for the neighbours to hear.

I speak to strangers, eat pizza for breakfast,
don't care who knows I am shameless, fancy
the entire Welsh rugby team – and I would,
if I could, Six Nations, most of them anyway.

But now?
Now,
now know this: every day since the funeral
I have worn your diamond engagement ring.

Walking the Back Road, After

The way the green lane opens for me,
stretches full length, often cranky,
but with arthritic fingered branches
beckoning, dry-tufted centre-parting
dividing the poor pock-marked tarmac
into uneven halves, my long absences
unremarked, no *Where have you been?*

even though I missed last summer's
sweetness, small scarlet strawberries
squashed alongside tractor-flattened
frogs, by morning all gone, no memory
of being magicked off into eternity
by carrion eaters in the dark velvet
hours below soft, star-stacked skies.

Then later, the way I see the fox left
on the hill vetch, that kill stretch,
where she lies low, grass verge hunched,
teeth bared, eyes missing, tyre tracks
if you look, though I can't, even when
winds ruffle autumn-fired fur to flick
the black-tipped brush back into life,

as if movement's all there is to living
and I think of you, unexpectedly quiet,
still, shape-shifted into chair-slumped
awkward, as though you've been knitted
on wrong size needles, dropped stitch
baggy, your violent vixen colours faded
from gilded ginger to silver grey, not

caring for appearances, vanity dropped
at the Care Home door, bagged up for
charity, those smart tailored suits,
fitted outfits made with your skilled
hands - someone else wears them now,
while I keep on walking the back road,
my eyes salted, trying not to unravel.

About the Author:

Originally from Worcestershire, poet and short story writer Louise G Cole has lived in rural Ireland since 2003.

She won the 2018 Hennessy Literary Award for Emerging Poetry and had a Dublin pub (temporarily!) re-named in her honour.

In 2019 Louise was selected by the then Poet Laureate Carol Ann Duffy for publication of a poetry pamphlet, 'Soft Touch' in the Laureate's Choice series, with poems endorsed by Jane Clarke, Dermot Bolger and Rita Ann Higgins.

Louise has had poetry and short stories published in anthologies, newspapers and literary magazines in the UK and Ireland, and has won or been placed in a number of local, national and international writing competitions.

Louise posts about creative writing at https://louisegcolewriter.com/ where she also explains the 'G' in her name is there to avoid unnecessary confusion with an underwear model.

'Under the Influence' was commended in Munster Literature Centre's 2021 Fool for Poetry Competition.

www.ingramcontent.com/pod-product-compliance
Lightning Source LLC
Chambersburg PA
CBHW021455080526
44588CB00009B/860